# SENIORS GUIDE TO CYBERSECURITY

# For 2021

Essential Cybersecurity defence Strategies and what everyone needs to know to protect themselves in an era of Cyberwar

## NATHAN
# JAMES

# Copyright

# Table of Contents

# Introduction

Every year companies, individuals, governments and companies all over the world lose billions of dollars to cyberattacks. Cyberattack is a deadly kind of attack, which can be targeted anonymously to various recipients to cripple their operations, steal their data, money or even frustrate them. Countries that have disagreements with others have been using this technological weapon to get back at their enemies without the victim knowing the exact attacker. This brings us to how to protect oneself against these cyberattacks, which can hit phones, computers, networks and every other digital tool capable of sending and receiving information.

The need for protection against these cyberattacks has led to the concept of cyber security and just as security forces and security institutions are created to defend a country from attacks, cyber security has been created to protect information technology tools from these cyber-attacks.

Part 1: Getting started with cyber security?

# Chapter 1

## What exactly is cyber security?

Cyber security is the practice of protecting information technology tools such as computers, network, telecommunication tools and digital data from attacks or harm that may eventually lead to its damage or malfunctioning. In other words, it is the act of guarding digital devices, their hardware and software components from simple, complicated or even deadly attacks that may lead to damage.

The importance of cyber security cannot be over emphasized. There are quite a lot of individuals, industries, businesses and government bodies that all have a need for cyber security in one way or the other because they all make use of these IT tools in storing, processing and transfer of information. Cyberattacks are often targeted at people or organizations because of fraudulent intention, personal disagreement or hate towards the company or individual although one can also fall into cyberattack traps set for others but it is important to know that these attacks are often intentional. Even government bodies around the world are not immune to cyberattacks since they can also be targets because of policies imposed by them that their citizens disagree with. War and armed conflict can also result in cyberattacks.

The changes in technology are the main reason cyber security is particularly important. These changes have affected many areas of human lives and the way we perform our day-to-day activities such as communication, work, travel and learning. This has inspired the creation of many technological devices, networks, and tools to help humans do things more efficiently, easier and faster. Although this comes with a lot of advantage, which has helped individuals greatly and made more business, thrive and make more profit. It also comes with a lot of disadvantages which is due to its vulnerabilities to cyberattacks. For example, social media technology is a type of technology that has changed the way the whole world works. A great majority of the human population on earth all have a social media presence where they can communicate with their friends and also learn about what's happening in parts of the world they may not be at the moment. Despite the fact that this technology has significantly driven the productivity of the world, it has numerous vulnerabilities because it contains the personal details of its users, which can be used to attack or destroy the person's image. Fraudsters now have a big market to shop for targets to defraud. This, among others, is the reason why cyber security has become an important case study.

Cyber security protects individuals from a couple of things, which include:

**1. Loss or damage of data:** whether in an individual's personal computer or an organization's data system, cyberattacks can be targeted at the data to either damage or clear it off their databases. This is the reason why many technological companies and websites backup their databases frequently to tackle this cyber threat before it even happens.

**2. Disruption of normal functioning:** some of these cyber threats are also created to disrupt the normal functioning of digital devices. When a device is hit with this kind of cyberattack, it begins to malfunction and often fails to carry out instructions sent to it.

**3. Information theft:** cyber security also protects from some cyberattacks targeted at stealing information from a company business or individual. Some of this information can be top company secrets that may cause a big breach in the security of the company or eventually lead to its bankruptcy.

**Common cyberattacks**

Cyberattacks have become numerous in the digital world as a result of the introduction of many companies, networks, websites and digital devices such as mobile phones and technologies. Some of the common cyberattacks one can encounter are:

**1. Malware:** its full term is malicious software and it is a class of cyberattack that often comes in specific software designs. This is the commonest cyberattack on computers, mobile phones and other digital equipment operators experience today. This type of cyberattack has been around for a very long time. Malware is a big concern to companies, businesses and even governments around the world as it can cripple their operations in no time when taken into the system. It is very difficult to avoid malware as some even come as email messages which when opened by the user can infect, spread to the whole computer and also infect other computers connected with each other. Its ability to spread quickly in a short time is a big issue that many antivirus programs and cyber-attack protection software have tried to tackle to little or no avail.

Malware comes in many forms and for one to defend and fight against it, one must be aware of the form it is attacking with. Below are some of the types of malware you should be aware of:

a. **Viruses**: this is a type of malware that replicates or multiplies itself into various files and programs of the computer system, which it has infected and alters them. Viruses can be gotten into the system through suspicious links, emails or even file downloads. It can also infect other computers running on the same network and also destroy the normal operation of that particular system. This type of malware is tricky and works by staying dormant in the computer system until the user eventually runs it knowingly or unknowingly. Running the computer virus then gives it more power to replicate and infect the computer legitimately. Computer viruses can be hard to remove from a system that has been seriously infected so it is necessary to know how to detect a virus on time. Some common signs of a virus infected computer are:

- Slow computer performance.
- Computer crashes.
- Loss of files.
- Insufficient storage space.
- Frequent strange pop-ups.

These, among others, are some symptoms of a computer virus. When detected, this virus should be dealt with using tested and trusted antivirus programs. You can prevent your computer from getting infected with this type of malware by always having up to date antivirus software in your computer system and clean the computer frequently. Also avoid opening random pop-up ads when operating the computer as some of these are ways to infect computer systems with viruses.

b. **Worms:** this type of malware is capable of replicating itself in the computer system and infecting other computer systems connected to the same network as well without being executed by the user as in the case of a virus. This kind of malware does not need to attach itself to files like viruses to operate in the system rather it comes in its own program. Worms remain hidden and unknown to the computer system until the results of the damage is being seen and experienced by the operator. This is because it takes roots in a part of the system where it cannot easily be discovered. The primary aim of a worm is to replicate itself, take up free space in the computer hardware, and eventually make it function slowly or even cause a crash. In addition, it can also delete files, make changes to the computer system, and slow down internet connection. To protect yourself from worms, do not download suspicious files or open emails you know nothing about. Common ways to detect the presence of a worm in a computer system are:

- Sluggish computer behavior.
- Frequent computer breakdown.
- Missing or altered files
- Automatic running of programs.

Once detected, worms can also be removed using antivirus software. Download tested and trusted antivirus software to clean out the worm.

c. **Ransom-ware:** this is a type of malware that hijacks a system's data or access to the system and only releases it when a ransom is paid to the attacker. This is similar to a kidnap situation where the victim is not released until a sum of money is paid. This type of software can get into a system through emails opened on that system. When this enters into the system, it encrypts and blocks access to files and programs in the computer. This denial of access can only be reversed by a secret code known only by the same attacker. Normally the attacker simply sends a message to the victim instructing him to send crypto currency payment to get the code to unlock the system. This type of ransom-ware attack is known as the encryption ransomware. Another type is one where the attacker down-loads and saves the victim's data on a database and threatens to release the data of the individual or company to the public unless a certain amount of money is paid by the user to an untraceable crypto currency account. This type of ransomware is known as leakware.

To protect yourself from a ransom-ware, switch on your firewall and avoid opening suspicious emails. For a user who is already infected by this malware, simply download a tested and trusted antivirus program and clean up the system.

d. **Trojan horses:** just like the harmless statue of a horse was used to break into the city of troy and destroy them, a Trojan horse is malicious software that hides in the guise of a legitimate file or program but its main aim is to destroy the computer, steal or alter its programs. This type of malware normally comes in the form of an email. One that seems familiar and poses to be from a friend or familiar recipient. By the time the user realizes he has been tricked into opening and downloading a Trojan malware into his system, it may be too late as the software may already start its self-replication sequence. Protect yourself from these programs by using firewalls to guard personal information. This type of malware can come to the system though a couple of ways but another way is through pop-up ads that may be advertising software or other products free to the user. This often is bait for the user to take.  Do not click on pop-ups you know nothing about.

Install tested and trusted anti malware software and protect yourself from Trojans or clean it from your system if already infected.

e. **Spyware**: this type of malware when it gets into your system gathers your financial, social media or other information from your internet usage and transfers it to unknown entities. In other words, your credit card and bank information, your passwords and very private information are the primary focus of a spyware. It gets into the system with the sole aim of monitoring the online behavior of the user like a spy. This is a threat to many businesses and individuals as some of these business transactions are done on the internet. Every year companies, individuals and companies lose a lot of money due to spyware that can give a third party access to another's personal and bank information. A way to detect when a computer has been infected with this type of virus is slow internet connection. Get antivirus software and clear it off your system as soon as possible.

**2. SQL Injection attack:** this is a type of cyberattack that affects the database of web applications or even websites and can delete or modify data in the database. It is a problem technological companies face often because it targets websites or web applications that rely on SQL databases. Examples of these databases include Oracle, MySQL and other SQL related databases. This is the ark enemy of web applications and is a major concern of many application developing companies and companies that own websites or applications since most rely on

SQL databases. Attackers inject SQL statements into databases to perform certain illegal queries, which eventually leave some information in the database missing or even transfer some of this information to the attacker. This means that information such as; customer information, passwords, credit card details are exposed in this process. SQL attackers usually look for vulnerability in entry points of the application or website. Therefore, one way to prevent an SQL injection attack is by getting programmers to protect all entry points to the application or websites.

3. **Eavesdropping attack:** just as the name implies, eavesdropping attack is a type of cyberattack that spies and listens to the victim's personal information such as passwords and login credentials. This type of attack is usually targeted at

people who use public networks. It can be used to hack virtual assistants such as Amazon Alexa, social media accounts such as Facebook and twitter. An eavesdropping attack can be tackled and prevented using firewalls, virtual private networks (VPNs) and also by having constantly updated antivirus software. Avoid clicking on suspicious links as they can also be used to eavesdrop on people.

**4. Password attack:** This is an attack on your computer that attempts to crack the password and gain access. It is not a type of attack that seeks to infect a computer with a kind of software to harm it rather; attackers try to gain access directly into a computer by working hard to break the password. It is why most websites require that users choose a strong password to make it difficult for the hacker to hack the password.

**5. Phishing attack:** This type of attack is one where the attacker comes to the user in the guise of a trusted friend, company or business through an email or any other form of message which contains a malicious link that may lead to serious damage to the system or even steal and modify private data from the system when clicked. This attack can result in fund theft and internet account theft.

There are various types of phishing attacks, which include:

a. **Spear phishing attack:** This type of attack seeks to gain access into a company's important network areas by targeting high profile individuals in the company with certain emails, which are somehow used to obtain the individual's login details and are used to gain access to the company's network.

b. **Whaling:** this type of phishing attack targets top executives in a company such as the CEO to steal important and private information from the company through them. These attackers are fully aware that these individuals are already used to handling other smaller cyberattacks since they might have received training about them. There-fore, they trick these individuals into making an authorization or make them click a link that looks like a trusted one and may benefit the company. This attack is to get the password and login details of these top executives in the company as it gives them access to the top position in the company's affairs where they can make some transact-ions that can profit them big time. These sizes of the targets are what make it a whaling phishing attack.

c. **Catfishing:** Catfishing is a type of phishing attack where the attacker uses the identity of another person to build a relationship with the victim on a social network and then use this relationship to defraud him or her. This is also known as a romance scam where the attacker earns the trust of his victim by proclaiming love and then defrauding the victim with this advantage.

d. **Clone phishing:** this is a type of phishing attack where attackers clone trusted emails to deceive the victim into clicking these emails, which will then be used to carry out malicious attacks. In this type of attack, attackers take advantage of the trust individuals have for emails they have received from reliable sources and then clone them while also adding malicious software which when clicked can be used to steal information from the victim.

**6. Denial of service (DoS) attack:** this is a type of cyberattack in which an attacker using a single computer system denies another user access to a network, system or internet service. This is usually done by interrupting the normal functioning of the system by connecting to the victim's IP address and sending excess requests to the system or network in a short time until it is too overwhelmed to even perform the instructions of its legitimate user. A DoS attack comes with symptoms such as:

- Slow system and network performance.
- Difficulty or denial of access to certain websites.

- Loss of internet and other device connections.

You can easily block the IP address requests receiving the excess requests to stop this DoS attack

**7. Distributed denial of service (DDoS) attack:** this is also similar to the DOS attack but is carried out by multiple computer systems, which target the same computer and overwhelm it with requests. This type of attack can be huge and frustrating since it completely cripples the system until the attack is countered. A DDoS attack makes a system experience certain symptoms such as:

- Extremely slow performance.
- Loss of internet or device connection.
- Uncontrollable amount of spam emails.

- Unusual heavy traffic.

DDoS is harder to stop than DoS because the attack does not come from one source. This type of attack is capable of sending gigabytes of information to a system in just a few minutes. Detecting the attack on time is a good way to quickly ward it off although you can call a DDoS mitigation specialist to help stop the attack when it has already been initiated.

8. **Adware:** this is a type of cyberattack that displays advertisements or pop up ads on a system in a very annoying manner that eventually becomes a big distraction. Adware usually comes into a system through downloaded files and software that contain adware or from a dangerous website infected with adware. It is called madware when it happens in a mobile device. An adware infected computer experiences symptoms such as:

- Slow system performance.
- Reduced memory as adware can take up much memory space.
- Longer loading time for photos, videos and files.
- Constant crashing.
- Slow internet connection.

Protecting against adware involves keeping an updated version of your system, ignoring or cancelling pop up ads, ignoring or deleting strange emails with links attached to them.

# Chapter 2

## The folk you must defend against

---

Bad guys are the attackers who deliberately plan and execute the cyberattack while accidental bad guys are individuals, staff who neglect and fail to take security precautions thereby carelessly bringing malware into the system which ends up infecting others in the same network. A cyberattack often cannot be executed unless triggered by the computer operator. It could be another user of the same WIFI Network or a staff member of an organization who acts as the accidental bad guy. These individuals are often unaware of the damage or consequences of their actions. In addition, this is one of the major problems of companies who employ staff. Bad and accidental bad guys can also be referred to as insider and outsider threats where the bad guys are the outside threats and the accidental bad guys are the insider threats. Sometimes insiders can cause more havoc than outsiders, since they have more access to the company's private information and may expose or leak them mistakenly.

**Some few bad guys to defend against:**

1. **Script kiddies:** these are amateurs in hacking who try to gain access to systems with the use of programs developed by other professional hackers. Script kiddies are often inexperienced hackers who may be relentless in trying to hack any system they can find.

2. **Corporate spies:** these are individuals who spy on business and companies in order to steal their business secrets or

to copy their methods without the company's knowledge. This is usually for the sake of giving that information to a competitor of that company. This act is known as computer espionage. The aim is achieved through various ways including hacking or introducing malware into the systems. Sometimes employees who do not feel happy about the job or feel they are not being treated right are the perpetrators of such acts in order to ruin the business as they leave. This is the reason it is important to always try to make your employees happy. You can also reduce the risk of falling for these corporate spies by monitoring your employees closely. Also, make sure to restrict access to places in your organization where top secrets are located and use two-step verification methods with very

strong passwords for important computer systems.

3. **Hactivists:** these are individuals who
   use hacking as a tool to fight against
   political enemies. These individuals
   generally unite to perform some cyberattacks in support or opposition to a
   political cause. Hacktivists also target
   organizations and institutions most of
   the time to send them strong messages
   by damaging some of their cyber
   infrastructure. One strong hacktivist
   group is known as **anonymous** and it
   has successfully engaged in this type of
   cyberattack over the years by sometimes sending DDoS attacks to it's
   target's website to disrupt user access.

**Handling non-malicious threats**

While it is easy to tag an attack bad and
intentional, some may not be intentional

and can happen based on human error or external disasters.

1. **Human error:** this refers to actions or inactions not intended to cause harm but end up enabling a security attack to take place. This type of situation is often classified under an accidental attack, as the individuals did not intend for the attack to take place. Some of these human errors in cyber security include:

- Downloading malicious email attachments.
- Using weak passwords.
- Sending vital information to wrong recipients.
- Wrong network settings that could lead to easy network access.

2. **External disasters:** this is also something one cannot control. Occurrences such as earthquakes, tornadoes, hurri-

canes could attack the victim. While these can have devastating effects and cost the victim serious physical damage, it can only be called an accidental attack as it is beyond human control.

**How to protect yourself against intruders**

a. **Update your system regularly:** whenever there is an update for your computer, do not hesitate to get the new version for your system. Some of these updates come with up to date protection and firewalls against some of the cyberattacks one may experience.

b. **Use stronger passwords:** the importance of using stronger passwords cannot be over emphasized especially in internet related accounts such as social media and emails. Using a stronger password can secure an account and make it very difficult for bad guys to break through. Changing passwords when an unusual activity is detected in an account or system is also a quick precaution one can take in protecting against bad guys.

c. **Avoid using public WIFI networks:** this is one of the mediums bad guys take advantage of to cause harm to their targets. A private WIFI network is a better option for a computer that contains your personal and important information. You can also set up a guest network and connect some other basic devices to it. This way, your important devices are connected to the private network while others are on the guest network hence attacks made on the guest network cannot do much harm to your computer or other important things since it is connected to a different network.

# Defending against accidental intruders

a. One way to tackle this problem is by teaching staff about security measures of the company and creating awareness about cyber threats they are likely to encounter. This is to ensure more carefulness on their part.

b. Bring to their notice latest cyber threats and latest ways they could be targeted and how to detect suspicious emails as this is the commonest way cyber attackers can get to them.

c. Staff, employees and individuals should also use stronger passwords in their accounts and avoid habits like writing these passwords down on paper.

# Part 2: Improving your personal security

# Chapter 3

## Evaluating your current cyber security posture

---

Cyber security posture refers to the general security of the individual or company. It is the overall defense that has been put up to fight against cyber-attacks. This tells an organization or individual where it stands and where to start its fight against new cyberattacks.

Getting a good evaluation of security posture involves identifying areas of insecurity.

### Identifying penetrations points

1. **Your home computers:** this is the computer used at home. A home computer to an individual may serve as much purpose as he wishes including being used

to log in to his email accounts, browsing through his social media accounts across different platforms. Basically, a home computer can be used both for official and personal purposes unlike an office computer that may be restricted from being able to view other things aside work related. This multiple use of a home computer leaves it to many attacks since it contains more information a hacker may need especially if it doesn't have antivirus software.

2. **Your mobile devices:** your mobile devices, which are also used to browse the internet and even click on bad links, may also be insecure to cyber-attacks. Mobile devices contain a lot of data including photos, videos, important conversations, app information and contacts. All these are information

that can be targeted by a hacker. A mobile device is vulnerable to attack if the password or lock method is weak. A third party for instance can easily open pattern lock in android devices. In addition, some of the most visited websites by mobile devices contain dangers such as malware and hackers that may target your mobile phone security. Data leak is often caused by mobile users who simply allow perm-issions to websites and apps without verifying the authenticity of the website.

3. **Your gaming systems:** Your gaming system can also be vulnerable to insecurity since they can connect to the internet and be used to compete with other players. This makes the user insecure as a hacker can hack into the

gaming software and steal private information.

4. **Your internet of things:** the inter connection and use of various smart electronic devices which are internet enabled and used to share and receive information known as IoT is also insecure against cyberattacks as it does not contain adequate defence against cyberattacks. Security apps such as antivirus are usually not present in such devices and this makes them more vulnerable.

5. **Your network equipment:** a connection to your network equipment can pose risk to your security as it can be used to break into your system.

This cyber security posture also encompasses all areas including; physical, hardware, software, network and even service providers.

A further step in evaluating cyber security posture is by answering some important questions such as;

- How safe is the organization from cyberattacks?
- How complex is our security system?
- How up to date is our security system?
- How can we fight against cyberattacks when attacked?

Answering this question already gives you an idea of how strong or weak your organization's security is.

Further understanding cybersecurity posture of yourself and organization will require that you take a look at the following areas:

1. **Network:** this is the connections of the systems and computers, servers in the organizations and how they share data

with each other. This is where the attacks usually come from and oftentimes it acts on the insider's ignorance.

2. **Physical security:** this is the visible and hardware security of the organization. Evaluating this involves checking if your server room keys are strong enough to keep intruders from breaking in and stealing or infiltrating the network of the company or even stealing data. It is also a look at how you store files in the organization and weather they are secure enough. Attackers may trigger attacks just to get to the files or records in order to destroy them with fire or steal them to avoid evidence. This is also a look at the strength of your cabinets and storage boxes.

3. **Security education:** this is how well the staff and individuals connected know

about cyber security. Securing a company is not just about building firewalls, downloading antivirus but also educating every other person about cyber security.

After this evaluation, the next step to take is how to improve the security of the organization.

**Some ways to improve the security of the organization are:**

1. **By getting up to date antivirus software:** getting an antivirus is not the final solution, as one also needs to update it so the versions are up to date with the most recent technologies. This is important because just as antivirus companies create new versions of this software, cyber attackers also create new methods to carry out their attacks.

2. **Backing up your data:** although you could single handedly tackle and fight against cyberattacks but records may be lost in the process even if you win the fight. This makes it important to always backup your data to avoid starting over again or losing very important information that may lead to loss of money.

# Chapter 4

## Strengthening physical security

Physical security is also important when it comes to cyber security and it is a defense that can help improve your cyber security efforts. Physical things such as cameras and smart locks are important in an organization.

Below are some ways to enhance physical security:

**1. Install HD cameras:** oftentimes, companies focus on the digital and network side of cyber security ignoring these physical aspects. Some cyber attackers may come take a look at the organization in person before carrying out their attacks. These attackers check the weak points of the company during such visits to know where to penetrate. Installing cameras in strategic positions can enable the security personnel to notice their foul movements and investigate them. Cameras can also provide evidence for legal purposes. Cyber attackers can also come to steal hardware like computers to get information from it. This type of attack may not necessarily come from an outsider but can come from an insider in the organization. A camera is a very reliable tool to get the perpetrator of such acts.

**2. Build smart doors and locks:** in organizations, there should be restrictions of movement. There are places only the staff and trusted officials should be allowed to go to and such places can be made more secure by building these smart locks, which can only allow access with the use of certain devices or keys available only to authorized staff.

**4. Protect and maintain the server rooms:** this is the central place for the connections of all networks in the organization so it is a place where only few high ranking individuals in the company or trusted staff should be allowed to get into. Attacks from the server room can have devastating effects on the whole organization. The server room should also be maintained and checked regularly for any damage or vulnerable points where attackers can come through.

**3. Install alarms:** when an unauthorized person goes to an off limit area, the alarm gives a signal. This is very effective to keep intruders out of some important places or prevent them from touching some crucial tools, files or physical material.

**4. Prepare for natural disasters:** while taking other areas of physical security into consideration, also don't forget about the unforeseen circumstances and natural disasters such as lightning, earthquakes, flood and fire that could also affect a cybersecurity efforts. All these can also lead to loss of data or destruction of vital hardware components of the company. In the case of lightning bolts, which can destroy some data in the database, earthing the company physically could be a solution to this problem as it prevents lightning from causing much damage to the physical components of the company.

**5. Educating employees:** teaching employees about cyber security is also an important thing to do to enhance physical security since they would also have access to computers on the network. Some of these employees may accedentally expose certain information about the company not knowing its damage. Making them understand this is also further strengthening physical security

These are awesome building blocks to place your cyber security on. Having a solid cyber security also involves having a solid physical security.

# Part 3: Preventing yourself from Dropping Your Guard

# Chapter 5

## Securing your accounts

---

Securing your accounts makes it harder for attackers to penetrate easily. Sometimes the little things we neglect such as; choosing strong passwords, login out of other devices are the leverage attackers use to attack. As individuals or businesses who use the internet or digital devices to communicate and carry out transactions, we must realize that we are targets of cyberattacks at all times.

 Below are some steps to help secure your account:

1. **Choose a stronger password:** Having it in mind that these attackers are very intelligent individuals who can break through certain things is enough reason to make your passwords a little

complicated so one cannot easily guess it. Use both upper and lower case letters as password and also include some numbers and symbols to make it more secure.

2. **Use your computer for your operations:** do not always make use of the computers of others to perform your operations as this can give them access to some of your sensitive information. Remember that insiders do some of the deadliest attacks.

3. **Avoid using the same password on all platforms:** So many individuals prefer using a password in all their accounts. This can be easy to do instead of trying to remember certain passwords all the time although it can be very dangerous. This does not keep an individual's account safe in the end since the attacker only needs to get one password to

access all other accounts of the individual. A good way to safely use different passwords on different accounts without forgetting them is by selecting accounts into two categories – the most important and the less important. Use a stronger password on the former and a regular password on the latter for easy remembrance. You can further secure your various accounts by using unique passwords for unique accounts. Also, learn to keep passwords private, avoid writing down passwords in public on paper as you could misplace this record, and risk your account safety.

4. **Update your devices and software:** develop the habit of following updates consistently as these updates come with added security features and up to date technology that can be used to fight against cyberattacks.

5. **Conduct business with reputable parties:** some attackers can also come in the guise of doing business to get into their victim's systems and carry out their malicious attacks so it is important to take note of business parties when doing business with them.

6. **Use official apps and websites:** not every online presence deserves to be explored even if they are recommended by other business partners. Only explore apps and websites that are official and authentic online presence.

7. **Do not install software from parties you don't trust:** some of the software installed on systems are the primary carriers of malwares and viruses that may cause havoc along the line after being installed. Avoid installing any software from any random source. Only

install from sources you have thoroughly investigated.

8. **Disclose only little information about yourself:** We do know how exciting it can be to post about our adventures and lifestyle on social media to get the likes. This can be hard for people not to do. Avoid posting too much about yourself on these public platforms as attackers can get more information on how to attack from some of the information you share.

9. **Use two or three step verification for your accounts:** This is a kind of security system where a user has to answer certain questions or perform certain tasks he alone is aware of to gain access into his account. It could be entering a verification code sent to a phone number or answering a secret question. This further makes it hard

for attackers to gain access since they also have to pass through this process to gain full access to the account.

10. **Use a payment method that eliminates the need to share credit card numbers with vendors:** hackers can trick users by posing as payment gateways and prompt the user to make a payment in which they ask for your credit card details in order to hijack and gain access to your account. Opt in for a more secure payment method that does not ask for credit card numbers.

11. **Always lock up your devices and accounts:** Avoid using automatic login processes, which can give anybody, easy access to your information. Rather always program your computer, mobile devices, account to ask for the password to gain access.

12. **Avoid clicking on suspicious links and pop-ups:** In your email, social media, or work accounts, do not click on just any link you come across even if it was sent to you by a very good friend. This is one of the easiest way to collect account credentials from unsuspecting users.

13. **Do not perform sensitive tasks over public WI-FI:** some things should not be done on a public network where an eavesdropper can easily spy on your operation and take sensitive information. A sensitive task such as trading in the stock market or login into your bitcoin wallet should not be done over a public network. You can easily read the news using such networks but do not log in to your accounts. Your accounts should only be accessed when you are in a safe location.

14. **Protect your cell phone number:** this is as important as it can get. Your phone number may be tied to a couple of things including your accounts. Do not easily disclose your phone number to anybody that asks for it especially strangers as this can be used to attack you.

**Passwords**

Passwords are the personal codes known only by the user to confirm his identity. Using a weak password for an account is like locking a room containing valuables with a sewing thread, which can be broken into with little effort. There are various consequences, which come with using a weak password, and some of them include:

- Gaining access to your bank account and making purchases in your name.

- Getting into your email and accessing private information.
- Using your identity on social media platforms and viewing your conversations.
- Accessing the information on your computer.

The use of a strong password is therefore important in protecting your account and identity. Some tips to creating a strong password are:

- Password length is very important so choose at least 10 characters, which may include letters, numbers and symbols in upper and lower case.
- Your password should not be a name or word directly associated with you like your name, date of birth, family member's name or hobby. Hackers usually start with the things around their victim and use them to guess

what their passwords could possibly be.

- Do not use ascending (123457) or descending (54321) numbers as your password. Do not also use similar numbers like 2222. Randomly choose the numbers for stronger effect.

**Some safety tips to keep you password safe and secret after creation:**

- After creating a strong password, avoid writing them down in a place where others can easily gain access and if you have to write them down, write it in such a way that you alone can understand what you wrote.
- One could be in a cafe and decide to access his account from there. Make sure not to leave your account logged in on these devices.
- Do not share your passwords with anybody via messages, as this can be

a record that may be used against you in the future. Password buying and selling is a lucrative business and a friend may sell your login details anonymously to an attacker without your knowledge.

- Know when to change your password: if you feel your password may have been compromised or spied on by somebody, do not hesitate to change it to keep your account secure.

- Do not click hurriedly on suspicious links even though they seem like trusted websites. Some links are traps by hackers for you to visit and input your password and details while they wait at the other end of the website to collect them. Study the link carefully before clicking.

There are also other secure ways to guard accounts from intruders, which can also be as effective as or even more effective than password. They include:

- **Biometric authentication:** this is a type of gateway security that takes the physical or behavioral features of a person and matches them with the saved reference to give him access. Biometrics authentication can be installed in other places such as cars and doors. Some of the physical human features that can be used for biometrics are fingerprints, eyes, voice, facial details and movement patterns. How this works is that the biometric data references, which have been stored by the user, are matched with the users login inputs to give him access when it matches correctly. Biometrics cannot easily be hacked into unlike passwords. The only way to gain access is by physically collecting the person's biometrics and using it to access the account. While it is easy to collect one's fingerprints, one's eyeballs cannot be collected.

Biometrics authentication comes with quite a lot of advantages and disadvantages. One of the disadvantages is the fact that the account may not be accessible if the person or the biometric used is no longer available. Unfortunate events happen which may lead to damage of that part of the body, which was previously used to access the account.

- **SMS based authentication:** this is a kind of access method where an SMS containing a code is sent to the phone number provided by the authentic user of the account, which is then submitted to gain access. This is a two-factor authentication. And it further keeps your account safe since the hacker cannot easily have your password and phone number at the same time.

- **App based one-time passwords:** this is another type of two-factor authentication where an app is used to get a one-time code, which can be used for only a limited time after which it expires. This method is a much more secure two-factor verification.
- **Hardware token authentication:** this is a little handy device with a screen and a little button which when pressed, it displays codes that can be used as tokens to login to the account they are tied to. This device incre-

ases security but is prone to theft as it can be stolen and used to gain access to the owner's account after hacking the password.

## Preventing social engineering

Social engineering is the process of tricking individuals into providing personal information such as passwords and bank details. Humans are often vulnerable to the tactics used in getting this information from them. Attackers act on the emotions of these individuals such as greed and fear. For instance, an ad displaying the sale of a popular product for a very low price may trick one into clicking the link that follows which will then be used to collect some of his confidential information. In this case, the emotion of greed made the individual fall for the attack. Another example is an email message telling the user that his password on a certain account is not safe and needs to be changed. The individual out of fear clicks the link that follows and then provides his old password in the process of choosing a new one. In this case, the emotion of fear made the individual fall for the trick. Perpetrators of such attacks can also act on the trust of their victim to get their information. For instance an email from a friend cannot be ignored but the victim may fail to realize that his friend may have been hacked or it is a cloned email message.

**Types of social engineering attacks**

1. **Baiting:** baiting, similar to phishing, is a type of attack that comes up with outrageous offers and acts on the greed of the individual to lure him into falling for the bait. The attacker in this type of attack normally promises the user some kind of rew-ard performing

an action such as login into their accounts. The user then logs in which in this process is nothing more than surrendering his login credentials to them through the fake website. Baiting also acts on the curiosity of humans to carry out this act.

2. **Scareware:** this is a type of attack that makes the user believe out of fear that they have to visit certain websites, download or buy certain software which often is loaded with malware to infect the user's system. It comes in the form of a warning in most cases. For instance, it may be a pop up which tells the customer about an infection on his computer and how it can be prevented by clicking on a link or downloading certain software. This makes users scared and eager to protect their sys-

tem when they are actually being attacked.

3. **Tailgating:** is a type of social engineering where an unauthorized person gains access into an organization's restricted areas by following closely behind an authorized person who is also going through that way. This works in a way that the authorized person cannot question the intruders because they may look like technicians who act very busy struggling with some boxes and making it look as though they simply needed someone to help them open the door to get in with their boxes or tools. Courtesy prevents the authorized person from questioning these intruders because it looks like they are genuine from the outside. In this case, attackers rely on the kindness of their victim to achieve their

aim. Tailgating can be a big security issue when the organization is a large one comprising a large number of employees. In this case, entry of intruders cannot easily be detected.

4. **Vishing:** this is the use of voice calls to trick users into providing personal information such as account or credit card details. The commonest vishing attack is one related to your bank where the caller claims there might be something wrong with your account and needs to be fixed immediately which will then require that you provide your login details or account information. People often fall for this social engineering attack because a phone call may seem more serious and authentic than a message or pop up. A vishing attack can easily be detected by

its need for urgency and the caller's request for personal information.

5. **Pretexting:** this is a type of social engineering attack where attackers pose as legitimate individuals in important positions who then come up with a story to get the user's personal information. The social engineer in this case creates a scenario in which the victim is then convinced to release personal information.

## How to prevent social engineering

- Carefully observe emails before clicking the links on them or downloading any attachments they may contain. If the email is coming from a trusted friend, you can confirm from them through other ways about the email before clicking on it. Chances are they may not be aware of such a message.

- Avoid outrageous offers: Do not click on ads that come with pictures and texts you do not understand. Often-times, some ads may come on your display claiming you are a winner or give you cheap offers. Do not click on these ads as they can be a medium to download malicious software to your computer.
- Avoid providing too much inform-ation about yourself on public plat-forms: The perpetrators of such att-acks usually gather information abo-ut their victims to know their weak points and where to attack them. Avoid providing the following inform-ation on social media:
  - Your schedule and travel plans: this information can be used to attack you and know the timing to strike.

- Financial information: even if you are a rich person, posting about your wealth on social media attracts dangerous individuals to yourself. These individuals can then make you their target.
- Personal information: you should keep your personal information a secret. The internet is a place that never forgets and such information can be used against you in the future when you may be running for a leadership position or even used to blackmail you.
- Work information: posting information like this on social media also leaves your work vulnerable to attack as they can use you as an insider to get to the company.

- Medical or legal advice: legal advice should be kept secret from the public to avoid it being used against you. Also exposing medical information such as the state of one's health can attract mockery.
- Your location: leaves you vulnerable to physical attacks and exposes your privacy and you may no longer be anonymous

- Do not get too familiar with strangers on public platforms: this is for the type of social engineering where victims engage in romantic relationships with strangers from distant lands and are defrauded along the line. The perpetrator of such acts first builds trust with their victim with the sole intention to extort money from them while hiding under the guise of love.

Avoid providing personal details to strangers on the internet, as you never can tell what the stranger's intention may be.

- Get tested and trusted antivirus software and update it as new versions are released. Also automatically scan your system each time you login to keep your system refreshed.

- Challenge suspicious strangers: in a physical office environment, it is important to question some few people who you feel do not belong to the organization. This helps in detecting intruders whose motive may be to tailgate employees to gain access into the company's vital areas and cause harm.

# Part 4: Cybersecurity for Big and Small businesses/organizations

# Chapter 6

## Securing your small business

---

Small businesses receive more cyber threats than big business. This is because big businesses already have solid security systems that may be difficult to break into while small businesses don't.

Small businesses face some of the commonest and deadliest cyberattacks, which include phishing, malware, and ransomware attacks.

Securing a business can help it grow faster and make more profit. It can save the business from loss that may arise as a result of cyberattacks.

### How to secure your small business

1. **Use stronger passwords for all accounts in your business:** A strong pass-

word is a strong fortress that can't easily be broken into. When creating passwords, make sure it is a combination of upper and lower case letters with numbers and symbols. The total character should be up to or more than 10 for a stronger password.

2. **Set restrictions on certain places:** do not allow just anybody to get to some areas of your business such as the server room. Restrict access to some computer systems and information to authorized individuals only.

3. **Monitor employees:** after setting the rules, make sure to always keep an eye on your employees to ensure they abide by the rules put in place.

4. **Incentivize employees:** ensure to motivate and encourage your employees frequently to make them more connected to you.

5. **Install surveillance cameras in important places:** secure the physical aspect of your business by installing a camera to watch the activities of your business. A camera can protect from hardware theft and also monitor suspicious movements around the business premises.

6. **Educate employees in security precautions:** employees have access to a lot of information about your business so it is very important to train them in cyber security. Training your employees can save you from data exposure and other cyberattacks. They should be aware of the ways an attacker can get to them and what to do when faced with such attacks. Training your employees also strengthens the security posture of your small business.

7. **Use the latest versions of software:** get the latest versions for your operating

system, browser, antivirus software and the important software you often make use of. These new software usually come with new ways to fight against new cyber threats.

8. **Enable firewalls** on your computer or download free firewalls to prevent unauthorized access to private data on your system through the internet.

9. **Backup your data**: Malwares can be very quick to delete or modify data when in a system so it is important to frequently backup your data in a safe place to prevent complete data loss when an attack comes.

10. **Secure your WIFI network**: Ensure to use stronger passwords to secure your WIFI from being hacked. Also, prevent the wireless access point or router from broadcasting your network name. This will hide it from bad guys.

11. **Use HTTPS for your website:** this is a security setting that only allows the system access to secure sites using the https protocol.

12. **Consider cyber insurance:** this is a type of insurance that protects your business from cyber threats such as data breach, malware and hackers. It is a good way to protect businesses from bankruptcy after an unfortunate event that cripples the business and its operations happens. This type of insurance can help you recover loss of data, income and also ransom payment in the case of a ransomware situation.

**Cybersecurity and big business**

Any organization whether big or small that connects to the internet is vulnerable to cyberattacks. These attacks do not leave the big companies and businesses out of their target although they may find it a little bit difficult to penetrate some big businesses who invest heavily in security.

Big businesses employ a lot of individuals and just as this can be one of the biggest assets the company can invest in, it can also be one of the biggest threats to cyber security in such organizations. Investing in firewalls, antivirus software and all sorts of cyber security does not make a big business immune to cyberattacks. One weakness a big business can have is when its employees know little about cyber security. This makes it very important for big businesses to consider educating their staff on cyber security after taking other security measures for their efforts not to be in vain. Some other reasons employees could be a threat to a company are:

- **Emotional issues:** Emotion swing is a cause of some of the cyber security problems big business face. Employees could get angry, sad, or over excited and make decisions based on these emotions that may ruin the security of the company.
- **Imperfections:** Humans often make mistakes and it is the same for your employees as well.
- **Disloyalty and maliciousness:** Some employees can have ulterior motives toward the company and take some actions that can cripple the business.

It is important to note that most of the challenges employees give are accidental and unintentional therefore, it is important for the business owners to constantly educate their employees on cyber security, encourage, treat them well, and supervise them.

The importance of cyber security in big businesses is as serious as it can get. Sometimes, hackers only need little information about a company to ruin its image or achieve their aim. Breaking into the company's database and accessing private information alone can destroy the image of the company since its customers may begin to fear that their personal data has been compromised. There are always people willing to buy these data gotten from a company on the dark web making it imperative for big businesses to update and change their passwords as often as possible.

**Some types of cyberattacks big businesses often face**

- **Ransomware:** This is a type of attack where the attacker breaks in, takes hold of certain important files or blocks access to a system, and then makes the company an offer to pay a certain amount of money in order to get access back to these files. This cyberattack is one of the most common attacks big businesses face. The ransom demanded is usually based on their size and the revenue they generate. The file or link usually comes from supposed legitimate emails, which then delivers the malware into the computer. People often fall for these ransomware attacks because they fail to back up their data often, hence the need to desperately get it back by paying the ransom. Attackers often look at how their victim values their data before attacking. For instance, a computer containing the family photos and other very important files is a target to cyber criminals if the owner has no backup.

Big businesses can prevent ransom-
ware attacks by:
- Backing up frequently.
- Avoid clicking suspicious links.
- Using antivirus software.

- **Insider threats:** as stated earlier, this
  is another major type of security attack
  big business faces. When an employee's
  action causes cyber harm to the business. Educating the employees and
  creating awareness to prevent actions
  of ignorance on their part is a way to
  tackle this problem.

All these and more are reasons why every
big business should have a competent
and experienced chief information security officer (CISO) to manage some of
these problems. The CISO is an individual responsible for a company's information and data security and some of his
roles include the following:

- **Overall system program management:** this is studying ahead and knowing the needs of the company as related to security and putting in place programs to manage those security needs before they even arise.
- **Fraud prevention:** a CISO prevents fraud from happening in an organization by putting in place programs to detect some deceptive transactions and prevent them from happening thereby protecting both the organization and customer involved.
- **Data loss prevention:** this is the protection of data from loss by setting backup systems and preventing backup failure. This is one of the primary roles of a CISO.
- **Investigations:** in the case where a breach happened, a CISO joins hands with other cyber security

professionals such as the forensics analyst to study the incidence.

- **Physical security:** physical security is also a vital plan of information security so it is also a part of the CISO's role to ensure that physical security equipment such as cameras, secure doors and keys, are put in place to increase the strength of security in the organization.

- **Incident response plan:** the CISO also puts in place detailed plans to help tackle and react to security breaches when they occur.

# Part 5: Handling a security incident (It is a case of when, not if)

# Chapter 7

## Identifying a security breach

Knowing what to do is one thing, while knowing when to do it is another. It takes individuals and small businesses a little time to detect a security breach, but takes big companies longer time to detect it and by then the damage may have been done. There may have been some symptoms during this period that were ignored and taken for normal system behavior. These symptoms are good indicators of security breaches and should not be overlooked. The best time to take action against cyber threats is the earliest stages of this security breach. This is the period when the malware or virus is at its infant stage.

## How to identify a security breach

Identifying a security breach starts with studying the normal behavior of the system and observing if there are any abnormalities. These abnormalities are symptoms, which point out an underlying problem.

It could sometimes be hard to detect a security breach but when you are experiencing it, you will no doubt see some of these things happening;

- You experience unusual slow operation of the system. The system suddenly takes a lot of time to respond to simple instructions and requires that you keep refreshing it.
- You experience reduced device storage space. This is one of the symptoms of a malware and its ability to replicate itself over empty space is

the reason it often consumes a lot of space thereby leading to reduced storage space.

- Multiple login attempts.
- Slow internet connection.
- Strange new files and software in the system.
- Your task manager doesn't run.
- Your system settings change all of a sudden. You could even see your system proxy change when you never set up one.
- Your device batteries, which used to last for a long time, begin to drain faster.
- The temperature of your system changes quickly and it begins to get hotter.
- You discover that files are missing from your folders.

- In the case of a DDoS attack, you begin to experience unbelievable traffic on your system in very little time.
- Security programs go off leaving the system as defenseless as a sheep.
- Frequent crashes on your device begin to occur on your device.

Business owners, employees need to be alert always and know how to detect these symptoms on time and take immediate action once detected.

**Recovering from a security breach**

Some cyberattacks are more severe than others are and can take the victim longer to recover. It sometimes matters on the preparation these individuals and businesses put in place against these cyberattacks before the attack happened. A well prepared organization with backups and an active security team can recover from an attack almost immediately without much damage. The preparation against cyberattacks before it happens gives a better edge against the attack than preparing and fighting when the cyberattack is ongoing.

Preparation is much more important in meeting these attacks head on than the best strategies to fight it when it has already happened.

Some security breaches can have devastating effects on the victims. Some may lead to bankruptcy while others may drag down the progress of the company significantly. An example is the case of one of the largest internet technology companies in the world – Yahoo, which experienced the largest security breach ever recorded in which all its 3 billion user accounts were affected. This unfortunately cost the company the trust of its customers as the majority of them left the company for good and this drastically reduced the company's worth. A security breach is not however the end of the world and can be recovered from by simply taking some steps listed below:

- **Do not panic:** for some this may seem like their whole world is crashing right in front of them. Do not panic when you start experiencing such an attack. Stay calm and apply wisdom to your next actions.

- **Be aware of the kind of attack you are experiencing:** figure out what is happening to your systems and use these symptoms to know what kind of attack this is to know the kind of measures to take against it.

- **Stop and terminate the attack:** Recovering from an attack starts from how to respond when in a security breach. One cannot recover when the attack is still in progress. You can stop the attack by first disconnecting the attacker's access to the systems and networks. If they gained access through a certain system, withdraw the system from the rest of the systems. In the case of a network, disconnect or reverse their access from the network. This way you can focus on fixing the damage that has already been done. In the case of a type of malware, you need to delete the whole or affected files assuming it has not done much damage to your files then recover the deleted files from a backup of your data. This works when there is a backup of the data otherwise the data may be lost. A backup makes recovery easier.

- **Studying how the attack happened and preparing for future attacks:** Get to know how they gained access to your systems and accounts. If it was through an email or public network. Knowing this will help you prevent such attacks from happening again. Attackers can come a second time during your recovery process and in this case, you must have been prepared to tackle and prevent them.

- **Recover and restore data:** in the midst of the attack, you may have been forced to erase all your data or the attack may have eaten everything up and left you with bits of your data. After stopping the attack, backup and restore your data including all your apps, settings and contacts.

- **Rebuild the system:** gradually rebuild the system by downloading the latest antivirus software and some other security software that will protect you from further cyberattacks such as this in the future.

- **Reaching out to those affected**: Your friends may have received unusual messages from your hacked account or system. Sometimes, the aim of the hackers is to tarnish the image of their victims by sending messages the original owner of the account cannot send to customers or friends. When the attack has been stopped, reach out and communicate in honesty with the people who may have been affected by the breach.

- **Learn from the mistakes**: This will give you an experience in dealing with such situations in the future. As you recover from the breach, also begin to take precautions you formally neglected in the past like backing up your data always. This will make you stronger against cyberattacks.

- **Set new security policies**: Set better security policies in your organization and make security a priority in your business.

- **Remain positive and optimistic**: Turn the tides to favor you and your business by using the knowledge gotten from the challenge of the security breach to build a better and more secure business.

Part 6: backing up Files and recovery

# Chapter 8

## Backing up Important Data and Resetting Device

The importance of data backup in almost all areas of human endeavors cannot be neglected as it is saved from a total loss of days, weeks, months and even years of data. Every business organization, individual or institution should have a backup plan as their first step to building a good business. Backup is simply keeping a copy or copies of data separately in order to recover them after the original gets lost, damaged or stolen. Backup is great business continuity tools that can enable any business to continue its normal transactions and operation even after loss of data.

Backup comes with so many advantages, which include:

- **Not negotiating with attackers:** In the case of a ransomware, where an attacker requests a ransom to get back your data for which you have a backup, you can simply overlook and go ahead to format your whole system and wipe it clean so you can have enough storage space to restore your data.

- **Fast data recovery:** A back up can save you the stress of having to start gathering and compiling years of information you have lost. Some of this information could mean the lives of a person in the medical field while it can also mean top secret of organizations and even countries. You can simply download everything from the backup and move on as though nothing happened.

- **Peace of mind:** It gives you peace of mind to focus on your business or endeavor and look for ways to make more profit.
- **Benefit to the customers:** a backup can also save the customer from losing important data such as pictures, videos and important files and documents uploaded to the company.

Data backup can further be classified into two main types which are; online and offline backup. An online backup is a type of backup where one can upload data on some backup servers while connected to the internet while an offline backup simply requires transferring files to an external storage device like a hard disk, memory card. Choosing a backup strategy may be hard because both methods come with their advantages and disadvantages.

## Advantages of online backup

- Online backing can be safer and less prone to data loss that may come from physical damage of the storage devices since it is safely stored in servers on the internet.
- Online backup can automatically update frequently as programmed by the user.
- The storage capacity is unlimited, which means more space for more data.

## Disadvantages of online backup

- Online backup is costlier and requires an active internet connection to perform.
- Online backup includes uploading your data to a cloud platform, which can encounter sudden crashes, disasters or cyberattacks when you might need the data most.

- Coupled with network unreliability and cost of internet access, you also have to pay to back up your data on these servers.

**Advantages of offline backup**

- Offline backup is much cheaper. Storage devices such as external hard disks and memory cards are cheap and can be easily accessible.
- Offline backup gives total control over your data and you can decide who sees your data.
- You do not have to pay to back up your data.

**Disadvantages of offline backup**

- Offline backup can easily be lost if not well kept by the individual. The storage devices can also get damaged physically which may also lead to loss of data.

- Offline backup requires manually backing up the storage frequently and adding new data which may be time consuming and stressful.
- Storage capacity may become limited as the devices collect more data.

An online backup may be the best option for a company with more data and an offline backup may also be the best option for a small business or personal backup. They can also be used together in the sense that some data can be backed up using online based cloud platforms while others can be backed up using offline devices. This is by far the best approach to backing up data.

Choosing which works for you is the first step to backing up your data.

## Exploring the right backup tools

These are tools used to perform backups to a local drive or disk. These tools have made it easier for offline backup methods as it can now be programmed to perform backup at specific timings. While some are free, others require payment.

Below is a list of some backup tools you can choose from:

1. Paragon backup and recovery.
2. EaseUS Todo backup.
3. FBackup.
4. AOMEI backupper standard.
5. Cobian Backup.
6. FileFort backup.
7. Backup maker.
8. DriveImage XML.
9. Comodo Backup.
10. Everyday auto backup.

## Smartphone/Tablet backup

The need to also backup files and data on smartphones is also rising since the use of these smart phones has increased greatly within a short period. More people now communicate with their mobile phones than on other devices and these saved contacts, passwords, files, settings and even accounts are prone to loss if not backed up. It could be a disaster if there is no backup for all that information. This kind of loss of data can cost the user his peace of mind, money and sometimes, contacts of lifelong friends. Smartphone backup is very easy and fun to do. Majority of phones can be backed up using google accounts although others also come with their backup methods.

## How to backup with a google account

- Go to **settings.**
- Choose **backup and reset.** This option can be found in different places in different phones. It can either be found in the system, **personal** or **account** option.
- The backup includes your apps and apps data, call history, contacts, device settings, photos, videos and SMS.
- Turn backup on to proceed.
- Select the google account to backup with and proceed with the instructions to complete your backup.

Your phone will perform a backup automatically according to how frequent you have chosen it to backup.

Backing up using other phone accounts such as Samsung is similar to the google backup.

Simply go to settings,

- Choose backup and restore
- Click on the **backup my data** to switch it on.
- Sign in to your phone account.
- Follow the instructions to backup

**Resetting your device**

A reset is a restoration of a device to its normal state. There are two kinds of reset namely – soft reset and factory reset.

**Soft reset**

A soft reset is a type of system function that enables the system to reboot itself to enable it to start running afresh. A soft reset is a troubleshooting tool and is usually done when an operating system is experiencing operating problems such as sluggishness, network problems and general temporal malfunctioning of the operating system. A soft reset is also done when new software is being installed into a system. All unsaved data are usually cleared in a soft reset.

A soft reset can be done by clicking on the shut down or restart option from the start menu. When you click shut down, you have to switch it back on yourself and when you're restart, it automatically switches itself on. Either ways, it achieves the goal of restarting the system.

It can also be done manually by pressing, holding the power button on the system so it goes off, and then pressing it again to switch it back on. This is particularly helpful when an application or malfunction prevents you from selecting the reset options while the system is on. You can also achieve this aim by removing and inserting the battery back and then switch it on again. All these achieve the aim of resetting the system.

**Factory reset**

This is a type of reset that is performed to restore the system, its memory, software and hard drive back to the default and original settings of the manufacturer. This type of reset is usually done when all other methods of trouble-shooting has been tried to no avail.

Sometimes, after a cyberattack, there may be a need for a reset of the system to restore it back to normal. In this case, a factory reset is used. Note that this clears out and erases all of your files and data on the system including the malwares, viruses or any other malicious software although your files may be completely lost if you have no backup.

**How to factory reset your system**

Make sure to have a backup before performing this type of reset to avoid losing important files.

You can perform this action by:

- Clicking on the **start menu.**
- Select **settings.**
- Click on **update and security.**
- Select **recovery.**
- Click on **get started** to begin the process.
- Click on **remove everything** for thorough reset.
- Follow the instructions to start the reset process.

You can also achieve this same aim by typing **reset** on the search field in the start menu and clicking on **reset this PC** when the results display then click on **get started**.

Your system will restore to its original version after a factory reset so if you upgraded from window 8.0 to 8.1, a factory reset will return it to version 8.0 and you might need to upgrade it to the latest version after the reset.

**Restoring from backups**

After a reset, hard drive failure or disaster that led to a loss of data, restoring from backups is the next step to take. It however depends on your method of backup. You can simply connect your storage devices to your PC and restore your data if you use an offline backup method. In the case of an online backup, you can restore your backup by going to server settings in the control panel of your cloud account and choose the backup you want to restore.

# Part 7: Future Preventive Measures

# Chapter 9

## Pursuing a cybersecurity career

---

As the need for security in the cyber world increases, more cyber security professionals would be needed in the future to defend businesses, individuals, governments and companies from cyber-attacks. This is a career with endless opportunities as there would always be these attacks. There has been an increase in the need for these professionals as Industries and businesses ranging from health care, manufacturing, finance and education all look to hire sound cyber security professionals to protect them and their businesses from cyber breaches and threats.

Cyber security is a field that has so many specialties and positions that all work together to fight against these cyber-attacks. One person cannot simply know everything about cyber security, which is why several specialists must always work together.

Some specialties in cyber security include:

- **Cryptographer:** They create programs and systems to encrypt data in order to protect very private information and files from being accessed.
- **Cryptanalysts:** They decrypt data to gain access and also design systems that can prevent attacks.
- **Security analyst:** They study, analyze and maintain the security of the organization. They are responsible for giving directives to the staff and IT professionals as to the security measures to take in the organization.

- **Security architect:** They think as the hacker and predict the moves he might take to attack the company. This enables the security analysts to place roadblocks in those areas so the hackers have no room to penetrate the company. The work of a security analyst is usually tested by other authorized hackers known as ethical hackers who try to break into the system deliberately to test its strength against outside cyberattacks. Security architects are up to date about the latest technologies that can be used by cyber attackers to attack. Previous hackers usually make the best security architects.

- **Security software developer:** These professionals who are well grounded in software development are responsible for developing new and secure software and making changes to existing ones to make it more secure. They also have knowledge in computer security that enables them to block weak points in applications where attacks can come from. This makes them stand out from others as individuals, businesses and governments usually trust them more with software development.

- **Security engineer:** These are the builders. They design systems that can protect the data of the company from occurrences such as natural disasters, which may include fire and earthquake, or even malware attacks. A security engineer is also responsible for building systems such as firewalls and intrusion detection systems.

- **Security auditor:** these are the computer system and cyber security auditors who study the system of the organization, create thorough reports about the weakness or strength of the system, and point out the areas where there should be improvement and how it can be done.

- **Ethical hacker:** this is a hacker authorized by the company to try to break into the system security and information system just like an external hacker would. The ethical hackers then get to work trying to break in. He tries a lot of methods like penetration testing, tricking the employees into leaking sensitive data. This way after the test attack is done; the company can find more weak points to block to further make its cyber security system stronger and more defensive to cyberattack.

- **Security consultant:** this is a person who advises the company on security related issues, network, software and even physical security issues, which include installation of cameras, natural disasters. They also decide on the best security measures a company should take to better meet the needs of their customers. A security consultant can either work for a single company or for several clients offering them security advice.

- **Forensic analyst:** these are the individuals who take a look at digital evidence which are valuable to track suspects and detect crime. They are trained to be able to detect how an attack may have happened within the organization if it was an insider job.

- **Security manager:** These individuals handle emergencies, create and implement security policies and procedures and oversee the control of security budget, recruiting, developing and supervising security personnel to be able to handle security emergencies.

- **Chief information security officer (CISCO):** these are high-ranking individuals in cyber security who are responsible for the overall information security of the organization. These individuals are charged with creating programs that are useful in protecting against cyber threats that may come. Some other roles of the CISCO is; teaching the employees about security awareness and anticipating new ways attacks could come.

The list is endless so it requires knowing about all disciplines in cybersecurity and choosing works for you. However in order to stay relevant long enough, it will be wiser to learn skills that are in line with the latest technologies.

You don't necessarily need a degree to start a career in cyber security. Although you can also pursue a degree for the discipline in school but if you are in another career and just want to add cyber security as part of your profession, you should consider self-training. Cyber security can be self-taught which means you can learn various courses and specialties in cyber security personally and practice it until you become a professional. You can also get certification from participating in cyber security courses online to boost your qualification and make you rise quickly in the profession.

**Exploring popular Cybersecurity certifications**

- **CISSP:** the certified information systems security professional is an advanced certificate awarded to individuals who have passed the CISSP examination by the International information systems security certification consortium (ISC)[2]. For individuals to take this examination, they must have had a reasonable level of knowledge and experience in information security.

- **CISM:** This is the certified information security manager certification, which is given also to individuals who have become experts in information security by ISACA. Individuals who process this certification are trusted more with handling, protecting and managing the security information of a company. Taking up the examination for this certification requires up to 5 years of experience in some specific information security disciplines.

- **Security+:** this certification is given to an individual who has practical knowledge and experience in cryptography, network security and operational security.

**Emerging technologies and new threats**

The way we operate technological devices sometime ago is not the same way we do it now. This is because of a change in technology due to the emergence of new technological devices. More devices and networks are being created daily and some of these creations are naive to security risks. While creation of new technological devices and facilities come, it is usually with many advantages such as making communication easier, more efficient and more fun, and also many disadvantages and new threats. More things will soon be done via information technology mediums such as the internet, emails, and digital devices. Cars now use android software to aid their driving. This has also made them vulnerable to attacks since they can be hacked and controlled remotely. As more people also get access to the internet, this creates a big market for the cyberattack ers to shop for victims from.

The digitalization of money also comes with its own dose of threats, which can include hacking, and breaking into an individual's crypto currency wallet.

Other new technologies such as voice assistants can also come with weaknesses that can be used to infiltrate the system or network.

**Ways you can improve your cyber security without spending a fortune**

You may be wondering how to equip yourself and business with a good security posture to keep yourself safe from cyberattacks without spending so much. The first step to improve your cyber security is to understand that you remain a target as long as you access the internet from a device containing information. Below are some ways you can improve your cyber security without spending much:

1. Imbibe the security consciousness in yourself and your staff so you will

always be security conscious in the things you do.

2. Make registration using strong passwords necessary in your organization.

3. Avoid public WIFI networks on your computer as this can easily sell you out as a target.

4. Use VPNs to access the internet to avoid vulnerability of your device data.

5. Backup your data more often. This helps you keep your data safe somewhere in case an unexpected incidence occurs.

6. Use antivirus software to always clean the system.

7. Do not share your account details without anybody as they are your personal information and can be used against you at any time.

8. Hire professional users who will be able operate and implement some of the security policies into the system.

9. Encrypt some data: hide or block too many individual's access to some kind of files that are confidential to you. This will help you save information safely and prevent intruders from gaining unauthorized access to them.

10. Be aware of suspicious emails: since emails are very common tools cyber attackers make use of, look out for emails which are phishy and avoid opening them. Also, make sure to update your device software and make sure they are up to date.

## Lessons from Past major cyber security breaches

Learning from a bad occurrence is the surest way to improve from it and making sure it doesn't happen again. Some of these lessons often point out weakness, vulnerability and laziness on the company's part, which can be fixed. These lessons are from big cyber security breaches for instance the yahoo cyber security breaches which left all 3 billion yahoo accounts affected.

Below are a few of these lessons:

- Do not underestimate the impact of cyber security breaches. Although it may seem like the impact outwardly is limited but deep down, the real damage may be deeper.
- Hiring the right people when it comes to cyber security matters a lot in trying to recover from a cyberattack. Do not go ahead to hire an incompetent person because a position needs to be filled. Carefully do your research before filling these positions.

- Limit employee access to some very important data in the system as some of the most deadly attacks are by insiders who had access to vital information.
- Always backup data in the case of data in the case of data loss. This will help you recover from such a loss and keep your business running.
- Have a recovery plan in case of sudden occurrences such as disasters and unpredictable elements.
- Train employees about cyber security of the company and let them know how their actions can drag the whole effort to protect the company against cyber-attacks to the mud.
- Always test your device hacking vulnerability: test the company's system often if they are strong enough to counter against similar cyberattacks.

- Trust no one not even a friend when it comes to cyber security. Oftentimes trust has led many to click on links that were not from a friend but an attacker and it ended up in tears.

- Everyone is vulnerable to cyberattacks no matter your size. Size does not determine whether you may be attacked or not. As long as you send and receive information or enable people to send and receive information through the internet, you are vulnerable to cyberattacks.

- Plan ahead of time against these attackers. Do not plan how to fight while in the battlefield, rather plan about how to fight the battle before it actually begins.

# Chapter 10

## Ways to safely use public WIFI

- **Use VPNs**: This virtual private network lies in-between faultless which one can't let go of. These VPNs to protect user identifications that may be uploaded to a hacker as a result in the use of a public WIFI.

- **Turn WIFI off when not used**: do not leave your device connected to your WIFI even when not in use. Ensure to put it off after use.

- Use antivirus software: make sure your devices are always being scanned in order to clean off malwares and viruses that may have come because of public WIFI. the antivirus software can even detect these attacks as they come into your system.

- **Turn off file sharing and activate firewall:** this prevents hackers on the same network with you from sharing files infected with malware with you and also allows your system firewalls to protect the computer from unauthorized network access.
- **Only use public WIFI to browse unofficial platforms:** avoid checking your emails, bank accounts, crypto currency account and some other very private information when using these public networks.
- **Do not stay long on WIFI networks:** avoid staying too long on these networks to reduce the chances of your being hacked.
- **Use two-step verification:** this is an added security that only gives you access to your computer and accounts after the secret question has been

answered. This makes it harder for a password hacker to break into your account easily. With this, even if your password has been hacked when in a public network, your account can still be protected until you change the password.

- **Make sure the WIFI network is authentic:** if it's a business place, company, hotel, restaurant, ask some of the workers in that business if the particular WIFI is actually authentic. Sometimes hackers can create fake networks close to the original one and have people browsing on these networks while downloading their information.
- **Use HTTPS:** only browse sites with the https attribute. This makes only encrypted connections to the sites you visit.

A padlock on the web address can also indicate a secure website.

- **Do not click on any pop up ad**: this might be a way to further get you hooked.

# About the author

Nathan James is a consultant Cyber Security and risk Management analyst with over ten years of experience in Vulnerability Assessments and Penetration Testing. Nathan is also a Certified Red Team Professional.

He spent the past few years training individuals, businesses and schools around the world on how to stay ahead of the 'bad guys'. He is married with three two beautiful daughters.

Made in the USA
Las Vegas, NV
20 January 2021

16232679R00085